AF802629

Geo. Herriman's

KRAZY & IGNATZ

VOLUME ONE

1916

INTRODUCTION BY Bill Blackbeard

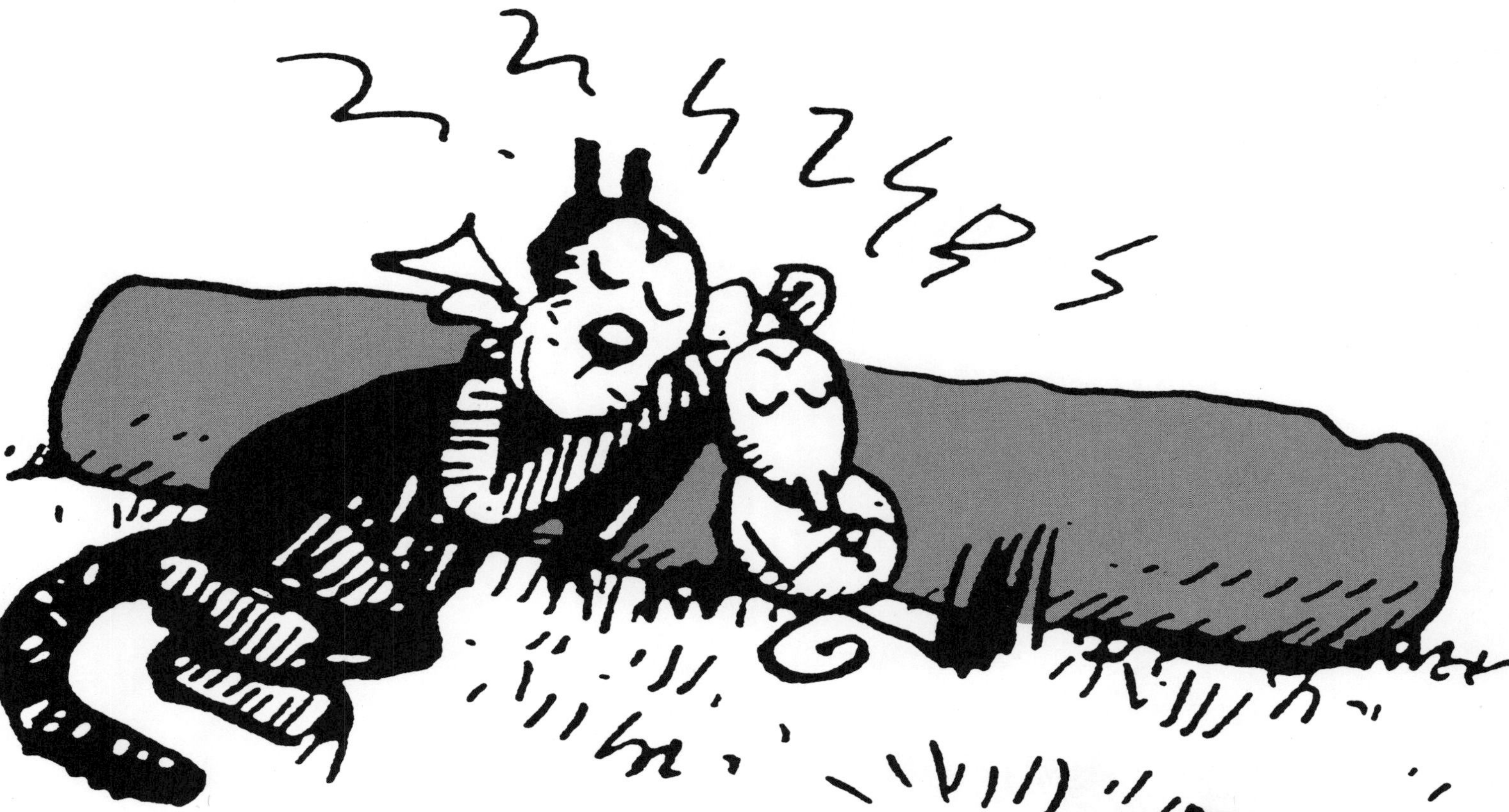

Eclipse Books / Turtle Island Foundation: 1988

Krazy & Ignatz is made available through a joint publishing effort by Eclipse Books and the Turtle Island Foundation. The book was conceived, and has been introduced by Bill Blackbeard, edited by Bob Callahan, designed by Dennis Gallagher, and produced by Cat Yronwode, Dean Mullaney and Associates at Eclipse Comics. Special thanks to Kathleen M. Cabana, Bibliographer, Reference and Bibliography Section, Library of Congress, Washington DC for copyright research connected with this volume. **Krazy & Ignatz** is available to the comic trade through Eclipse Books, PO Box 1099, Forestville, CA 95436. It is also available to retail book stores through the Subterranean Book Company, PO Box 10233, Eugene, OR 97440.

© 1988 Eclipse Books/
Turtle Island Foundation

0-913035-48-3 paperback, $9.95
0-913035-49-1 limited cloth, $29.95
Second Printing
Printed in Singapore through
Palace Press

*Krazy & Ignatz is dedicated to
the memory of Dori Seda.*

The Kat's Kreation

By Bill Blackbeard

In the Beginning, there was the Squiggle.

The Squiggle was lively and jet black and adorned with a white ribbon tied in a bow. Large goggly eyes made a burglar's mask out of a black cranium above a bewhiskered white muzzle. Usually set at a placid center amidst surrounding comic chaos, the squiggle was obviously a cat, a marginal visitor in many of the turn-of-the-century drawings of a young cartoonist named George Herriman.

Later, it was to become, forever, a kat.

Cat or kat, this masked feline was a figure Herriman clearly enjoyed drawing, turning up often enough in the artist's early work to justify being dubbed — one wonders if the thought occurred to Herriman — an actual mas-kat.

In and out of magazine gag panels and layouts, peeking from one-shot newspaper comic pages, the creature made its first full-fledged comic strip bow in Herriman's "Lariat Pete" Sunday half-page published by the T.C. McClure Syndicate in most papers on September 6, 1903.

In its first real adventure, the creature merely frolics on the outskirts of the central action, keeping serenely clear of the lunatic goings-on occurring at center-stage.

In the following week's episode, however, it finds itself the focal point of the hero's lariat action, maintaining its essential calm nevertheless (aside from a briefly erected tail which rises in the second panel of the episode). The cat's bland indifference to the boy dropped on it — any actual cat would have bolted in terror and anguish — certainly

LARIAT PETE. T.C. McCLURE SYNDICATE, 1903

The Birth of a Cat

In "Lariat Pete," for the first time, Herriman adds a small black cat to his gallery of players.

foreshadows the attitude of the Coconino Kat to come when later brick after brick sparks loving hearts from its forever dizzy head.

A few months later, we find this cat again, this time stalking a dog — not yet a bull pup — in still another Herriman half-page strip called "Bud Smith," drawn for the World Publishing Company, February 27, 1904. In this new strip, the taunting of the dog seems at first separate from the main action, but quickly comes to prove decisive to the climax of the episode as a whole.

Up to this point, the cat has appeared largely as a pantomime artist. Yet in another Herriman half-page from this period — "Rosy's Mama," dated September 3, 1906 — we find the creature engaged in actual conversation.

"Cat, I have a presentiment," a small pup says in the third panel, anticipating the final outcome of Rosy's adventure.

"Me too, Oh," responds the Cat, breaking its previous silence.

Kicked around in the last panel as expected, the pup complains directly to Rosy's irate father: "Aah, wot did I do?"

Wot did I do, indeed.

Herriman's animals have learned how to speak.

Anthropomorphism has entered the Herriman cosmos, never to leave.

Three months after "Rosy's Mama," Herriman tackled his first "cat" strip outright. The new cat was named "Zoo Zoo," and it appeared in a panel under its own name on the editorial page of the *Los Angeles Examiner* in November, 1906.

"Zoo Zoo" represented a fluffy reversal of a kind. Zoo Zoo, the cat, was snow white, with a black ribbon tied in a bow. The cat-who-will-be-krazy did not wait long, however, before also appearing in this strip.

In the episode which appeared in the *Examiner* on December 15, 1906, Zoo Zoo's devoted owners have left their pampered pet alone with a sumptuous banquet of goodies — and an open window leading directly to the back alley. Through the open window now pour a half dozen of the alley's best, including, of course, the cat-who-will-soon-be-krazy.

LARIAT PETE. T.C. McCLURE SYNDICATE, 1903

The visitors receive a royal welcome from lonely Zoo Zoo, ending their visit by venting their long-stored wrath upon a portrait of a much-hated family dog, "Zipp," a regular neighborhood terror — particularly, it seems, so far as local trash can-can dancers are concerned.

These "Zoo Zoo" panels are of particular importance to Herriman scholars. Published in 1906, they antedate by three years Herriman's "Daniel and Pansy" strip — the cartoon adventure previously regarded as Herriman's first all-animal strip.

Herriman would create still another "cat" strip in 1909.

This new strip was called "Alexander," and it appeared — courtesy of the World Color Printing Company — on December 19th of that year.

In its formal interiors and scrupulously repeated decor, "Alexander" contrasted amusingly with the great Kat strip soon to follow.

The fall of 1909 proved to be major turning point for George Herriman, and his later career as America's most imaginative comic strip artist.

During the fall of that year, Herriman was devoting most of his creative energies to the adventures of a certain "Baron Mooch," another new daily comic strip which appeared on the pages of the *Los Angeles Examiner*.

In the December 11, 1909 episode of that strip, we find the Baron applying for work at a boarding house run by a certain Mrs. Lillydale. Obviously having spent a few days between meals, the Baron is in the process of eating the kitchen parrot's bird food when something like magic takes place beneath his feet.

Our old friend the cat reappears, and so does a new duck-billed character known as "Gooseberry Sprigg."

"Oh sir," says the cat.

"Ah Kat," responds Gooseberry, "Were you not such a lowbrow, I would a tale unfold to you."

It is an altogether historic occasion.

A cat has been transformed into the kat right before our eyes.

The Cat Begins to Speak

In "Bud Smith" and "Rosy's Mama" (overleaf), Herriman's now familiar cat is given his first few lines of dialogue.

BUD SMITH. WORLD PUBLISHING COMPANY, 1904

BUD SMITH. WORLD PUBLISHING COMPANY, 1905

ROSY'S MAMA. WORLD PUBLISHING COMPANY, 1906

ROSY'S MAMA. WORLD PUBLISHING COMPANY, 1906

A recurrent romper along the fringes of Herriman's fancy, a cat has become the kat at last.

Six months later — and a continent removed from Los Angeles — the kat will reappear in Herriman's first *New York Journal* daily strip, "The Dingbat Family."

In the Dingbat episode for June 24, 1910, he can be found first in logo for that strip, sitting beside his beloved new master, E. Pluribus Dingbat.

He also makes a first appearance in the panels in the episode below.

"You don't seem to know who you're shovin, kat. Do you?," a small dog says to him in the strip's last panel.

"Ehn?," the kat responds, confusedly.

Cat to Kat, the die has been cast for good.

Over the course of the next few months, the kat now known as krazy — the mouse to be known as Ignatz will call him that, for the first time, on September 25, 1910 — can now be regularly found skittering around under the feet of the human principals who make up the Dingbat Family, battling, fleeing from, and being beaned regularly by an obstreperous mouse and an ebullient pup.

Pantomimic for a brief period, the kat and his new friends soon resort to acidic commentary, and then move on to more complex dialogue and action, ultimately receiving their own small daily panel structure running below the daily Dingbat Family adventures.

Indeed, by 1913, a regular "Krazy Kat" daily strip can be found on the pages of the *New York Journal*.

Readers are now able to turn from E. P. Dingbat's familial follies — or one of its many spin-off strips — to Krazy and Ignatz's daily bricknic on the very same *Journal* comic page.

The new "Krazy Kat" daily soon proved to be a great success with *Journal* readers. This early popularity seems to have resulted from the extreme simplicity of Herriman's art and gag structure.

The strip was virtually always just Krazy and Ignatz, with occasional walk-ons by the bull pup — still a few years from his badge and night stick —, Joe Stork, and a number of one-time characters.

Each day the kat and mouse would run through a vaudeville turn, a Burns and Allen kind of skit, with Ignatz playing the part of the angry straight man reacting to Krazy's mad off-the-wall insights and remarks.

During this period the strip looked and read like a cross between "Mutt and Jeff" and "Peanuts." The repetitive slapstick of the one and the easily grasped layout of the other proved enormously appealing to the reading public.

Anyone could follow the simple smart-stupid relationship of these two comic animals, enjoy the frequent punning punch lines, and quickly recognize the strip's passing references to politicians, writers, artists and actors then in the news.

Only at fleeting intervals — in occasional seizures of pure graphic and thematic inspiration — did the daily "Krazy Kat" of this period give more than a hint of the conceptual wonders of the strip it would become when it moved to the spaces allowed on Sunday's full and open page.

The sheer money-making appeal of Herriman's daily Kat adventures soon led the strip's publisher, William Randolph Hearst, to request a full page "Krazy Kat" for his Sunday papers.

It is unlikely, however, that Hearst had any inkling of the kind of work Herriman would now produce, his imagination sparked by the opportunity to return once again to work on a full-page newspaper canvas.

George Herriman's first Sunday Krazy and Ignatz pages must have sent shockwaves through the entire network of Hearst's various local editors. These first Sunday pages simply stunned the Hearst bureaucracy, who quickly yearned for the relative simplicity of the earlier daily strip.

Certainly the changes in the strip were startling.

Suddenly the relatively barren, previous Krazy strip was populated with dozens of new characters.

Numerous new animals crowded the

ZOO ZOO. *LOS ANGELES EXAMINER*, 1906

Herriman's First Cat Comic Strips

In "Zoo Zoo" (above) and "Alexander" (overleaf), Herriman creates his first comic strips in which a cat plays the role of the main character.

ALEXANDER. WORLD PUBLISHING COMPANY, 1909

scene, tumbling out of odd corners everywhere.

The off-and-on bull pup visitor of the daily strip became overnight a police officer in some sort of complex, functioning society, while the unadorned stage world of the weekday gag now sprouted a bewildering array of foliage and landscape, a fantastic, shifting three-dimensionality of a kind never before seen on a comic page.

Those first Krazy and Ignatz Sunday pages — as fresh and wondrous today as they were in 1916 — seemed to hit Mr. Hearst right where he lived.

William Randolph Hearst just adored his new Sunday "Krazy Kat" page.

However distorted he might seem at times by the exigencies of getting out a string of sensational dailies, Hearst's basic artistic instincts remained as sound as they had been back in 1889 when he corralled a visiting Thomas Nast to turn out a few dozen cartoons for his first newspaper in San Francisco.

He remained the same sound judge of talent he had been when he paid the brilliant Winsor McCay a good deal of money to draw a weekly "Little Nemo" page that baffled his readers, and lost his paper circulation dollars for a time in 1911.

Would Herriman's explosion of creative energy be lost on his regular readers as well?

Hearst solved this problem much as he solved that of McCay, with editorial adroitness and financial largesse.

Just as he had previously evicted "Little Nemo" in a hurry from his national four-page color comic section to reassure readers that pure slapstick and tomfoolery would once again prevail in those limited pages, only to add the strip to the color back page of his weekly magazine section where its admirers could still find it; so Hearst now cancelled plans to release the Sunday Krazy as a syndicated color feature, and placed it instead on an inside black and white page of the paper's national drama and art section.

Here, Hearst reasoned, the intelligentsia could find and appreciate Herriman's new experiment, while regular readers could read their vastly more simplified daily Kat undisturbed by the possibility that their favorite cartoonist had suddenly gone bats!

Unfortunately Hearst reckoned without the reaction of his local editors. Although the color comics and magazine sections of the Hearst papers were pre-printed for inclusion in the Sunday editions of the Hearst chain around the country, the contents of the Sunday drama and arts, and political sections were sent out as boilerplate (paper mats ready for reproduction), and remained somewhat subject to local editorial decision.

It wasn't long before editors in Chicago, in Boston, in Los Angeles or San Francisco, rebelled against the inclusion of a sizable Sunday "Krazy Kat" page every week in the limited pages of a section where readers would presumably prefer to find more coverage on locally released movies and local and visiting dramatic productions.

Numerous letters backed up these editors in their feelings. Complaints about "this weird stuff nobody can understand" began to arrive regularly in the mail.

And slowly, but surely, local editors began to grow weary of the time and money required in writing explanatory and agreeable replies to such people, particularly when the letter-writer in question might be a local advertiser complaining that the readers who were now skipping over these various "Krazy Kat" pages, might also be skipping over their own paid-for ad.

Finally, the local editors rebelled.

The new "Krazy Kat" page was regularly pulled from local editions — only to be restored just as quickly when Mr. Hearst noted its absence and demanded that it be reinstated at once.

This internecine battle raged on into the 1920s, and then ebbed as Hearst's interests now began to take a more cinematic direction.

By 1925, "Krazy Kat" had received the full critical adulation Hearst had always felt it would finally draw. In 1925, a major John Alden Carpenter ballet production based on the

BARON MOOCH. *LOS ANGELES EXAMINER*, 1909

A Cat Becomes The Kat

In "Baron Mooch" and "The Dingbat Family," Herriman begins to build his most famous character, transforming a mere cat into the legendary kat of historical record.

THE DINGBAT FAMILY. *NEW YORK JOURNAL*, 1910

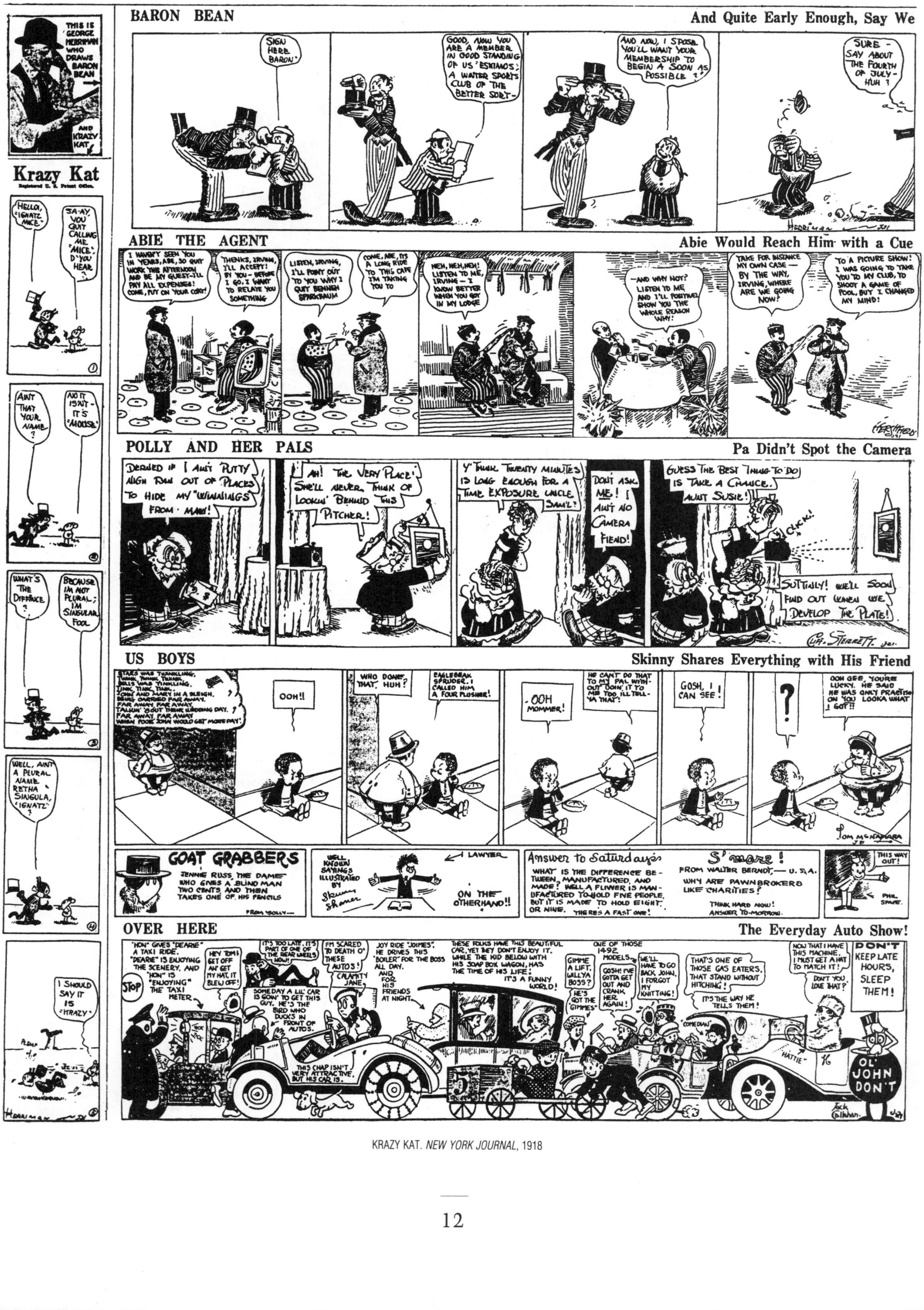

KRAZY KAT. *NEW YORK JOURNAL*, 1918

This Kat Is Krazy

The evolution now complete. Krazy Kat begins to appear in his own strip, first in daily panels, and later on his own Sunday page.

KRAZY KAT. DAILY PANEL, 1916

strip hit Broadway. Later that year the leading arts journal of the time, *Vanity Fair*, added Herriman to its contemporary Hall of Fame.

While the average reader might still scratch his head from time to time, for people like Pablo Picasso and e. e. cummings, Charlie Chaplin and Gertrude Stein, Sunday with Krazy and Ignatz had become a real thrill in a decade George Herriman had more or less made into his own.

As the work begins on these pages, "Krazy and Ignatz: The Komplete Kat Komics" offers the reader an altogether unprecedented opportunity. For the first time ever, beginning with this volume, and continuing each quarter with a new volume featuring a full year of Sunday work, the reader will be given a chance to read Herriman's most masterful strip in a consecutive manner. Insights and associations merely hinted at in previous random selections from this work take on full meaning as we witness the epic tale of Coconino County unfold week after week, year after year. The complete Sunday Krazy Kat is a visual record of extraordinary power, drama and delight.

The adventure, as they say, begins with this volume.

Krazy & Ignatz

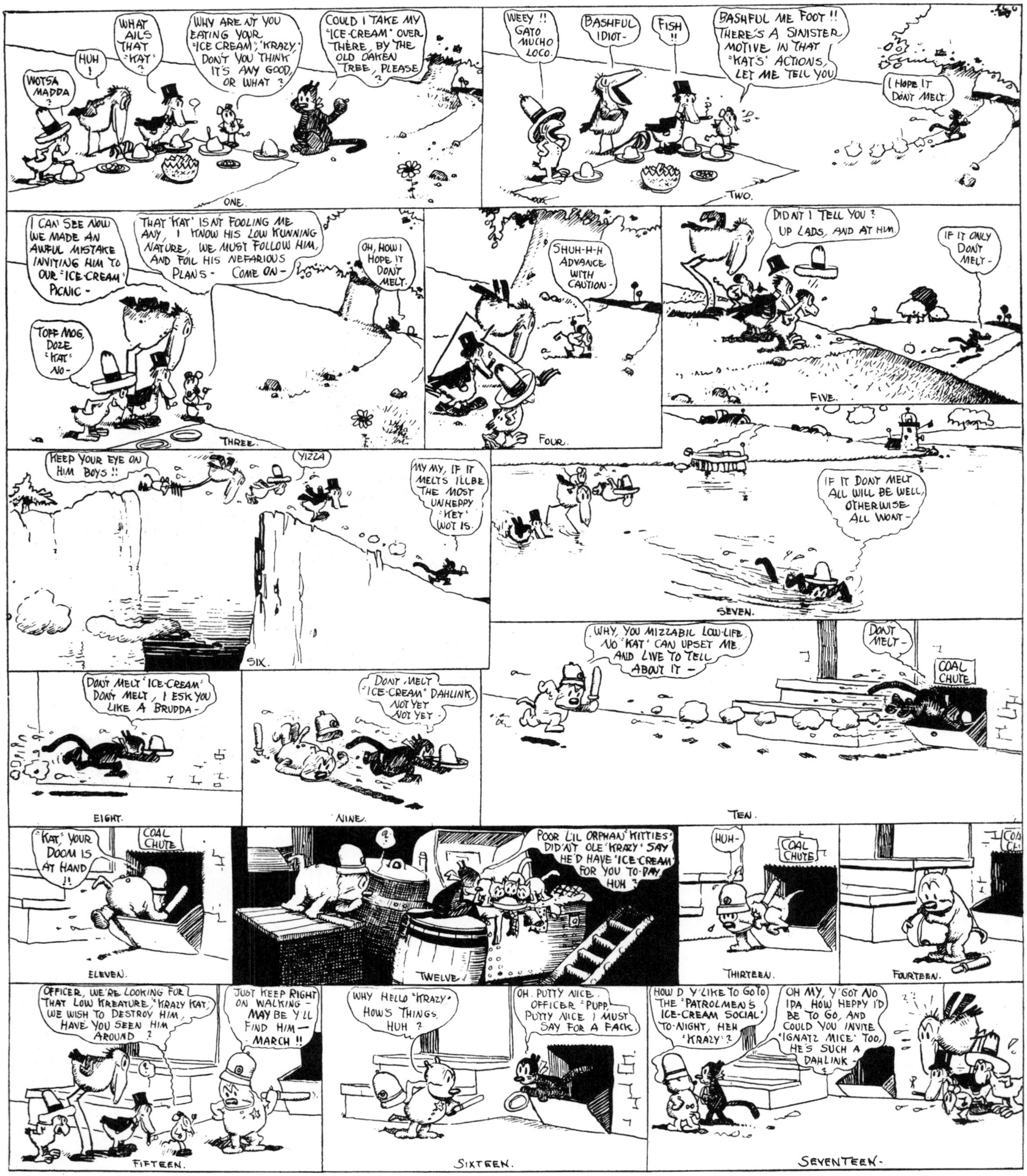

APRIL 23, 1916

APRIL 30, 1916

I MUST FIND THAT "KRAZY KAT". AND WHEN I DO, AH-H
ONE
KRAZ-EE-EE !!!
TWO
KRAZ-EE-EE-!!
THREE
?
FOUR
WHO DARES TO TELL ME, "GOOSEBERRY SPRIG" THE "DUCK DUKE" TO HALT !! HUH?
GO NO FARTHER "DUKE," AT YOUR PERIL -
FIVE
JUST AS LOUD AS YOU CAN, "DUKE"
KWA-A-A KWA-A-A
SIX
HEAR THAT - HUH - HEAR THAT ?
KWA-A-A-KWA-A-A
SEVEN
WHAT DO YOU MAKE OF IT, "DUKE"?
HOW SHOULD I KNOW, FOOL, MOVE OVER A BIT, AND GIVE ME SOME ROOM -
EIGHT
WHAT'S THAT ?
JUST YOU CALL OUT LOUD, AND YOU'LL SEE.
YOU SURELY WILL, SIR
NINE
BOW-WOW !!
TEN
SEE ?
SEE ?
I SEE
BOW WOW !
ELEVEN
?
?
?
TWELVE
I THINK I FORGOT SOMETHING, I-I-I'D BETTER GO BACK AND GET IT -
THIRTEEN
I THINK I DID TOO - UH - IN FACT I'M SURE I DID -
FOURTEEN
AH-HAH - HERE COMES "KRAZY"
FIFTEEN
I WONDER WHERE IS IT "IGNATZ" ?
SIXTEEN
HE'LL BE SCARED TO DEATH -
OH "IGNATZ" OOH-HOO -
SEVENTEEN
MY GOODNESS, LISTEN TO THAT "ECHO"
OH "IGNATZ" OOH-HOO -
EIGHTEEN
WELL, I GUESS I'D BETTER BE FINDING "IGNATZ" L'IL "AINJIL" -
NINETEEN
TWENTY
OLD SLOOTE
PLATO
ECHO
TWENTY-ONE
TWENTY-TWO
ZING
POW !
AH-H - AT LEST, MY DAHLINK IS HERE
TWENTY-THREE
A-A-AH - SHUT UP !!
A-A-AH SHUT UP !!
HERRIMAN
TWENTY-FOUR

MAY 7, 1916

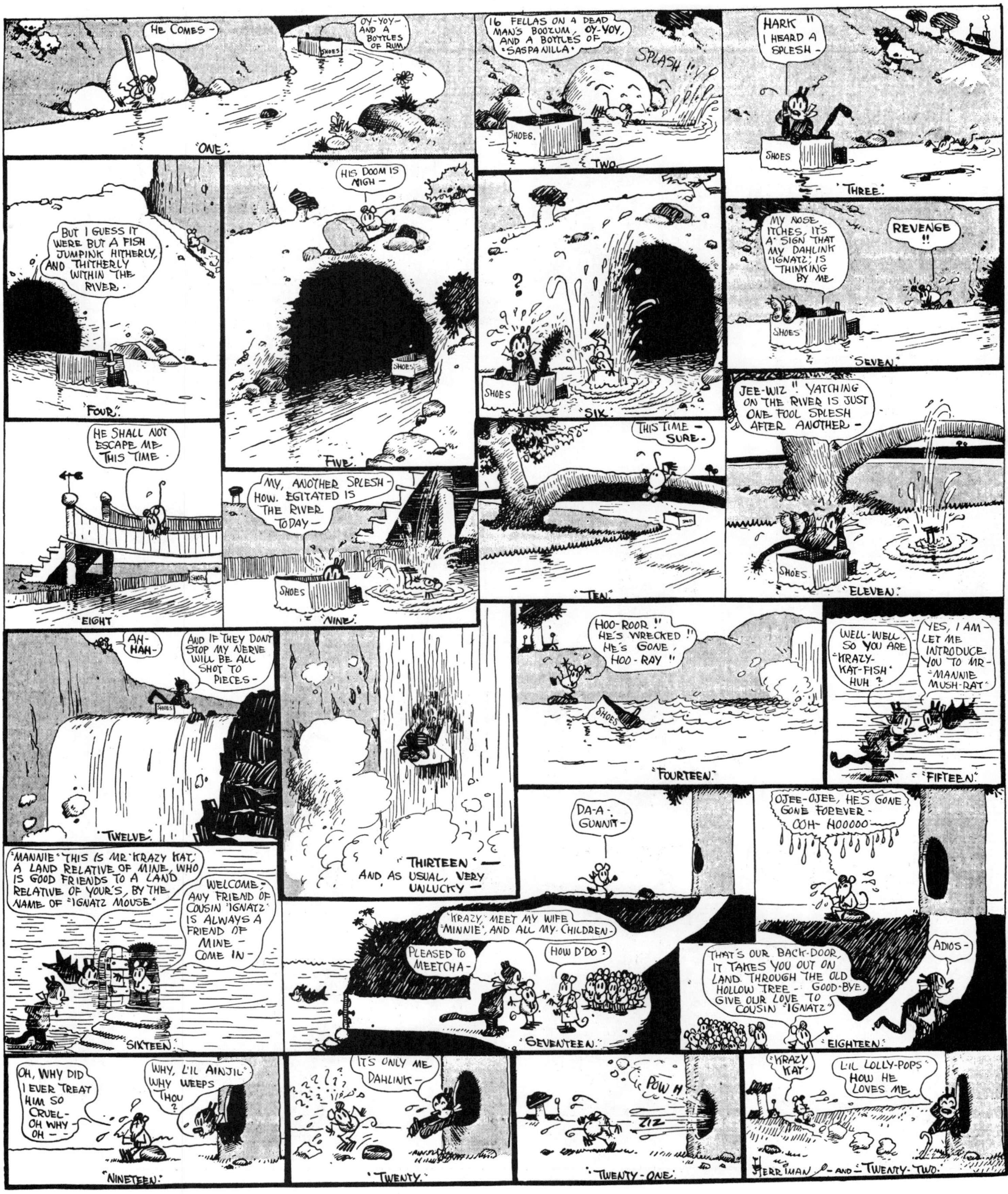
HE COMES -
OY-YOY - AND A BOTTLES OF RUM
SHOES
"ONE"
16 FELLAS ON A DEAD MAN'S BOOZUM, OY-YOY, AND A BOTTLES OF "SASPANILLA"
SPLASH !!
SHOES.
TWO.
HARK !! I HEARD A SPLESH -
SHOES
"THREE"
BUT I GUESS IT WERE BUT A FISH JUMPINK HITHERLY, AND THITHERLY WITHIN THE RIVER.
"FOUR"
HIS DOOM IS NIGH -
SHOES
"FIVE"
?
SHOES
SIX
MY NOSE ITCHES, IT'S A SIGN THAT MY DAHLINK "IGNATZ" IS THINKING BY ME
REVENGE !!
SHOES
"SEVEN"
HE SHALL NOT ESCAPE ME THIS TIME
SHOES
"EIGHT"
MY, ANOTHER SPLESH - HOW. EGITATED IS THE RIVER TODAY -
SHOES
"NINE"
THIS TIME - SURE -
"TEN"
JEE-WIZ !! YATCHING ON THE RIVER IS JUST ONE FOOL SPLESH AFTER ANOTHER -
SHOES.
"ELEVEN"
AH-HAH-
AND IF THEY DONT STOP MY NERVE WILL BE ALL SHOT TO PIECES -
SHOES
"TWELVE"
"THIRTEEN" - AND AS USUAL, VERY UNLUCKY -
HOO-ROOR !! HE'S WRECKED !! HE'S GONE, HOO-RAY !!
SHOES
"FOURTEEN"
WELL-WELL SO YOU ARE "KRAZY-KAT-FISH" HUH ?
YES, I AM - LET ME INTRODUCE YOU TO MR. "MANNIE MUSH-RAT"
"FIFTEEN"
"MANNIE" THIS IS MR. KRAZY KAT, A LAND RELATIVE OF MINE, WHO IS GOOD FRIENDS TO A LAND RELATIVE OF YOUR'S, BY THE NAME OF "IGNATZ MOUSE"
WELCOME - ANY FRIEND OF COUSIN "IGNATZ" IS ALWAYS A FRIEND OF MINE - COME IN -
SIXTEEN
DA-A-GUNNIT -
OJEE-OJEE, HE'S GONE - GONE FOREVER - OOH- HOOOOO -
"KRAZY," MEET MY WIFE "MINNIE", AND ALL MY CHILDREN -
PLEASED TO MEETCHA -
HOW D'DO ?
"SEVENTEEN"
THAT'S OUR BACK-DOOR, IT TAKES YOU OUT ON LAND THROUGH THE OLD HOLLOW TREE - GOOD-BYE GIVE OUR LOVE TO COUSIN "IGNATZ"
ADIOS -
EIGHTEEN
OH, WHY DID I EVER TREAT HIM SO CRUEL - OH WHY OH -
WHY, L'IL AINJIL WHY WEEPS THOU ?
"NINETEEN"
IT'S ONLY ME DAHLINK -
"TWENTY"
POW !!
ZIZ
"TWENTY-ONE"
"KRAZY KAT"
L'IL LOLLY-POPS HOW HE LOVES ME
HERRIMAN - AND - TWENTY-TWO

MAY 14, 1916

YOU GET HOLD OF "MANNIE MUSKRAT," "DINNY DOCKRAT," "PHIL. FIELDMOUSE," AND THAT POOR RELATIVE OF YOUR'S "CLARENCE CHURCHMOUSE," AND ALL MEET ME AT THE OLD "CLIFF" - I KNOW WHERE THERE'S A NEST OF "CANARY BIRD'S" EGGS, WE'LL GET 'EM, AND HAVE A FEAST, OR MY NAME IS'NT "WILLIE WEASEL" - HOW ABOUT IT, "IGNATZ"?
CANARY BIRDS EGGS IS MY DISH, EXACTLY-
THE COAST IS CLEAR-
THIS'LL BE MY FIRST MESS OF "CANARY" EGGS THIS SPRING, AND I THINK I'LL HAVE MINE POACHED-
SHIRRED FOR MINE.
MINE WILL BE SCRAMBLED.
FRIED-
HARD BOILED IS MY DISH-
?
I MUST FOIL THEM-
KANARY KOTTAGE
SHALL WE CHLOROFORM THE OLD BIRD IF SHE YELLS?
SH-H- NOT SO LOUD.
NO, IF SHE PUTS UP A HOLLER US FIVE HUSKIES OUGHT TO BE ABLE TO HANDLE HER - ALL RIGHT.
KANARY KOTTAGE
ROBBAS "TEEVES," THEY LITTLE SUSPECK THAT THEY GOT ME TO RECKON WITH-
KANARY KOTTAGE
POOY, SUCHA UGLY TAIL.
SURRENDA, WILLINS !!
WHY "IGNATZ," IS IT THEE?
YES, IT IS-
A CAT, A CAT, RUN FOR YOUR LIVES !!
SO IT IS-
YOU KNOW IT.
ZAP
OH-HOH, SO IT WAS THAT "CAT" WHAT CHASED THEM MICE AWAY, AND CHEATED ME OUT OF MY DINNER-
KANARY KOTTAGE
YOU SEEM DISTRESSED "KRAZY"
BUT I AINT, OFFICER "PUPP" I'M HEPPY, A LOTTA ROBBAS WAS ABOUT TO STEAL MRS. KANARY'S EGGS, BUT I FOILED THEM-
YA-AS, AND FOILED ME TOO, Y' IDIOT-
SOME DAY, I'LL FIND SOME THING TO GET MAD AT HIM FOR - THEN I'LL PINCH HIM-
ZIP
KANARY KOTTAGE
GOLLUX !!
I WISH THAT "CAT" WOULD GET AWAY, SO I COULD GET MY "DECOY SIGN," AND LURE THOSE "MICE" UP HERE AGAIN - I'M HUNGRY-
NO "IGNATZ," WE'LL STAY RIGHT HERE UNTIL MRS KANARY'S EGGS IS BIG ENOUGH TO TAKE CARE OF THEMSELVES-
L'L'LET'S GO AWAY FROM H-HERE "KRAZY"
SOON AS THAT "CAT" GOES AWAY, WE'LL TACKLE THEM "EGGS" AGAIN=
KANARY KOTTAGE
HERRIMAN.

MAY 21, 1916

AH, 'IGNATZ', YOU'VE GOT NO IDA, HOW MUCH I LONG TO BE A 'HERO'-
POO-POODLE: POO-POODLE: WHO EVER HEARD OF A 'KAT' BEING A 'HERO' ?
ONE.
WHY TO BE A 'HERO,' YOU'VE GOT TO BE LIKE 'NAPOLEON' AND 'ROMEO, AND JULIET', AND JOHN. L. SULLIVAN', AND VILLA', AND OLE CAPT. KIDD' - FULL OF FIGHT AND GINGER' -
TWO.
AND, AIN'T I LIKE THAT, 'IGNATZ' ?
NO
ZIZ
THREE.
PAP !!
ZEP
FOUR.
SO - MR. 'KAT', S'YOU-HUN ?
FIVE.
POW !!
ZEEP
SIX.
SEVEN.
EIGHT.
PAM !!
ZOP
NINE.
DAG NABYA !! NO 'KAT' CAN TRIFLE WITH ME LIKE THAT !!!
ZAP
TEN.
POW !!
JOWY
ELEVEN.
TWELVE.
AND THE NEXT TIME MR. 'KRAZY KAT' YOU SHY A 'DORNICK' AT ME - WA-AL YOUR WHOLE NINE LIVES WONT BE WORT 'THAT' - SAVVY ?
SNAP
THIRTEEN.
B-B-BUT OFFICER 'PUPP' I-I-I-
FOOL-
FOURTEEN.
I'M LETTING YOU OFF EASY THIS TIME 'KRAZY' BECAUSE IT'S YOUR FIRST OFFENSE, BUT DONT DO IT AGAIN - I'M A BA-A-AD BEAR' WHEN I'M INFURIATED, A BA-A-A-AD, BA-AAD BEAR' - YASSA !!
PLOOP
FIFTEEN.
SOFT SHELL
SIXTEEN.
I-I-I DID'NT ACT EXACKLY LIKE THEM NAPOLEONS; AND THEM OTHER FELLAS WOULD'A ACTED. DID I, 'IGNATZ' ?
I SHOULD SAY YOU DID NOT !!
SEVENTEEN.
ODEER, ODEER, THEN I GUESS I AIN'T NO 'HERO'-
EIGHTEEN.
HEY !! 'HERO' !!!!
HUH - I WONDER - I WONDER -
ME TOO -
HERRIMAN
NINETEEN.

MAY 28, 1916

NOW "KRAZY" YOU TAKE LITTLE "KATRINA" OUT FOR AN AIRING - BUT REMEMBER, NO LALLYGAGGING, NOR KOODAFOODLING AROUND WITH THAT BAD "MOUSE" "IGNATZ" D'YOU HEAR ?
YES, ENT TEBBY - VERRA WELL -
THE HOUR I SPEND BY YOU DEAR HEARTS, IS LIKE A STRING OF POILS TO ME-EEE -
HELLOA "KRAZY" LET'S PLAY "SPANIOLA"
OOH, I COULD'NT DO IT TODAY, "KETTAPILLA", 'CAUSE I GOTTA GIVE LI'L "KETRINA" HIS ERRING IN THE GO-BUGGY, AND EVEN WITH "IGNATZ," I CAN'T PLAY - SO ADIOSES
AH HAH
I CAH-HOUNT THEM EVER ONE A-PART - MY ROSY-REE MY-HY ROSY-REE -
A-AH SHUXLES !! WHAT'S THE USE OF HOMINY, MY HEART AINT MUSICAL WHEN "IGNATZ" AINT NIGH -
?
ZIP
NOW I KNOW WHY THEY CALL EM GO-BUGGIES
WHA-A-HOOOoou
MARY-ANN McCARTHY SHE WENT OUT TO DIG A CLAM -
!
AH GOO -
AH GOO ? I'LL AH-GOO YOU, Y'BAT-FACED CAT - I'LL AH-GOO YOU IN JAIL -
HOLD ! OFFISSA "PUPP" RESTRAIN YOUR-SELF !!
OH-HOH -
THERE "OFFISSA" IS ALL I GOT, SIX CENTS, AND A COLLA BUTTONS WHAT I WAS SAVING TO BUY FOR "IGNATZ" A BIRTHS-DAY PRESENT.
HAND IT OVER, THAT "MOUSE" CAN BUY HIS OWN PRESENTS
LOOK !! S'GONE A-GAIN !!
DOIND, IF IT AINT !!
HERE'S YOUR INFANT "MRS. TABBY" WHAT I FOUND.
I DO HOPE YOU WILL FORGIVE ME FOR THINKING YOU WERE A BAD "MOUSE," WON'T YOU ? - AND, OH, WON'T I PUNISH THAT "KRAZY" NEPHEW OF MINE WHEN HE GETS BACK -
YES, AND JUST GET ME A "BRICK," AND I'LL HELP YOU DO HIM UP -
SH-H HERE HE COMES
OH, WHAT'LL "ENT TEBBY" SAY - - ODEER, IF "IGNATZ" WAS ONLY HERE NOW TO COMFIT ME IN MY HOUR OF TEARS -
BOO-HOOO
HERRIMAN

JUNE 4, 1916

-JOE STORK, WHO LIVES ON THE "ENCHANTED MESA", GOES OUT, EARLY THIS MORNING -
- THE LUMP OF COAL IN THE CORNER IS "KRAZY-KAT" WHO WAS OUT LATE LAST NIGHT. -
KO-VADIS ?
-AND "KRAZY" IS AS FULL OF "KURIOSITY" AS ANY OF HIS TRIBE. -
AND.
IGNATZ MOUSE
NOW THAT HIS "KURIOSITY" IS SATISFIED, LET'S GO ON WITH THE "TALE"
FURNITURE
FURNITURE
A PERFECT "BRICK", A PERFECT "DAY" AND THAT "KAT" NO WHERE IN SIGHT -
ZIP -
AND, OH, YOU THOUGHTFUL MAN, YOU'VE BROUGHT THE LITTLE "DEARS" A LOVELY "GO-CART" -
SO THAT'S WHAT HIT ME - GOSH, I THOUGHT IT WAS A AUTOMOBILE.
HE'S AN IDEAL FATHER
WELL, I GUESS I MIGHT AS WELL INTRODUCE 'EM TO KELLY'S BRICK-YARD; NOTHING LIKE STARTING THEIR EDUCATION, YOUNG -
I WONDER WOULD HE LET ME BE A "NEAR-UNCLE" TO THEM - "LIL DAHLINKS"
HERRIMAN

JUNE 11, 1916

GRAFT
PFOO, NOW I'LL COVER IT UP, AND ADD ONE MORE "BONE" TO MY SAVINGS ACCOUNT.
STOP THIEF !! STOP THIEF !!
"DON" KIYOTE," THE MEXICAN BANDIT, OR DO MY EYE DECEIVE ME-
STOP THIEF !! PO-LICE POLICE !!
DUTY CALLS
STOP THIEF
OH, UNCLE "KRAZY" HOW KLEVER YOU ARE
YES L'IL KETRINA, I'M A PRETTY SMART "KET" - LISKEN, ONCE A LONG TIME A-GO THERE WAS LIVINK ON THIS "WOIL" ENIMALS BIG LIKE A HOUSE - THERE WAS "DINNY-SORRISES," "WEEGA-NODONS," "MEGA-PHONIUMS," "MEMMOTHS"-
AND GREAT BIG "LIZZIES," UH, I MEAN "LIZZIDS" WHAT WAS CALLED "ITCH-THYOSORRISES" BECAUSE THEY WAS GREAT SCRATCHERS OF GARDENS, AND THINGS, THEN THEY WAS BIG KANARY BIRDS WHAT WAS CALLED "PETER-DECKTILS" BUT A-LAS "KETRINA" ALL THEY IS LEFT OF THEM NOWADAYS IS THEIR "BONES" - JUST "BONES" - AIN'T THAT AWFIL ?
ODEER ODEER ODEER
AND LOOK, "BLESS ME ON MY SOUL," IF THERE AIN'T ONE THEM WERRA-WERRA "BONES" OF WHOM I WAS SPEAKING -
GAZE WELL UPON IT "KETRINA," BECAUSE FROM IT A GREAT-OLD AGE LOOKS AT YOU, ONCE IT WAS PART OF A "SABER-TOOTH" TIGA," NOW IT IS BUT A MERE "BONE," - AH HOW SUCH IS THE "WOIL" - A-LAS -
DON'T GET EXCITE, "KETRINA," S'ONLY "IGNATZ," HE'LL BRING THE "BONE" BECK, THE L'IL "AINJIL"
GIVE ME THAT "BONE"
GOOD HUNTING !!
YOU'RE GOING TO LEAVE THE WORLD BEHIND FOR A WHILE, "DON," ABOUT THREE MONTHS I SHOULD SAY.
SILENCE
MORE THAN THAT, IF I CAN FIX IT WITH THE "JUDGE"
WELL, I MIGHT AS WELL SLOW UP A BIT, I'VE OUT-DISTANCED THAT FOOL "KAT."
MY "SOUPER" !!
DA-AH-GUNYA !! I GOTCH YA !! HUH ? WITH THE "GOODS" ON, TOO-Y-SAYCAT !!
ONE SIDE, ONE SIDE I'M GOING A-WAY FROM HERE !!
HE'S GONE HE'S GONE !!
STOP THIEF STOP THIEF !!
AH-HAH-
SEE, "KETRINA," I SAID HE WOULD
AS GOOD AS A "BRICK"
KA-PLOP
ZAP
NOW, AS I WAS SAYINK "KETRINA," ABOUT THIS OLD "BONE" — MILLYINS OF YEARS AGO, BEFORE "CRISTOFUS COLUMBIA" DISCOVERED THE WORLD - ETC.
YES-YES "UNCLE" YES-YES
HERRIMAN

JUNE 18, 1916

DONG - BONG DONG
GLONG DONG
AH-H T'IS THE "HOUR OF THE BALCONY"
DONG 'LONG DONG
AND WHEN ALL THE WOIL MAKES LOVE, I SHOULD HAVE TO BE BAKING "TORTILLAS"
A MENDOLEEN -
PLINKITY PLINKA PLINKA TLING
ODBER, ODBER WERE ONLY IT "IGNATZ", WERE IT ONLY HE -
OH
OH-H THAT FACE, OH THAT FACE -
S'ONLY OLE "DON KIYOTE" PRETENDING TO MY MAIDEN "ENT TEBBY" - WHEN IT SHOULD HAVE BEEN MY DAHLINK "IGNATZ" -
I QUIT, DA-A-GUNNIT, I QUIT - THAT FACE HAS TAKEN ALL THE SONG OUT OF MY SOUL - THERE SHOULD BE A LAW AGIN SUCH FACES -
NOW, LET'S CUT BACK TO WHERE "KRAZY" LEFT THE "TORTILLA" SIMMERING INSIPIDLY UPON THE STOVE
OH-HOH "TORTILLA" - T'IS WELL !!
SNIFF
DONG GLONG DANG
NOT A "TORTILLA" ON THE STOVE, AND "KRAZY" NO WHERE IN SIGHT - OH THE LAZY, WORTHLESS, SCOUNDREL -
HE'S PROBABLY OUT IN THE YARD MOONING ABOUT AS USUAL, THE WAGABONE !!
AGAIN, WE CUT BACK TO WHERE WE LEFT "KRAZY" IN A STATE OF GLOOM UPON THE "BALCONY"
OH "KUPID" I AM THY WILLINK WICTIM - A - LAS -
OH-HOH EVIDENCE OF AN INTERRUPTED SERENADE.
T'IS HIM T'IS HIM -
I WONDER HOW ONE OF THESE THINGS IS PLAYED ?
FLINK !!
"IGNATZ" !! AINJIL !!
PLAP !!
ZAP
OH - S'YOU - HUH ?
OJEE, HOW HE LOVES ME - L'IL ADONIUS
I'M SO HEPPY I'M MIZZABIL - AH - WHAT A WONDERFUL THING IS "LOVE"
OH, SO THERE YOU ARE, HUH ?
YES "ENT TEBBY" - HERE I ARE, AND THAT'S A FACK.
SOON AS HE GETS A LITTLE DEEPER IN THAT TRANCE, THAT "TORTILLA" IS MINE AGAIN -
OH, FOR WHY MUST SUCHA PERFICK DAY END SO SOON ?
HERRIMAN

JUNE 25, 1916

① AND THE WIND RAISED UP IN THE SOU-SOU-WEST
AND TOSSED JIM: AND JOE: KOKOKNUTT OUT OF THEIR NEST.
=YEZZA.
THEY LOOK LIKE A COUPLE OF MOTHERLESS ORPHANS WITHOUT ANY DAD -
② AND THE VERY FIRST THING DID "UNCLE SUN" SEE
WHEN HE CAME UP FOR A BIT OF A 'LOOK AROUND'
WAS IT JIM: AND JOE: ROOSTING UP IN THE TREE ?
NO, NO THE L'IL KOKOKNUTT KIDS WERE DOWN ON THE GROUND.
-' BYRON '-
KELLY'S BRICK-YARD.
DON'T MISS HIM.
I NEVER DO.
③ MISTER 'KOLIN KELLY' RUNS A SWELL BRICK YARD
AND THE GOODS HE SELLS ARE TOUGH, AND HARD
=YOOBETT
THAT 'KAT' IS THE WORRY OF MY LIFE.
IGNATZ MOUSE, A YOUNG RODENT, CALM, AND SERENE,
④ WICKED, AND SINFUL, AND VICIOUS, AND MEAN,
ON HIS JOURNEY OF MISCHIEF HERE CAN BE SEEN,
FOR TO BEND A BIG BRICK OVER KRAZY KATS BEAN.
.KWITE SO =
KO-VADIS ? PHOES, OR ENEMIES ?
FT FT FT
⑤ A KWEER KAT IS 'KRAZY K.'
A SIMPLE SOUL IS HE.
HE'S GOT THE BRAINS OF A GNAT
TUCKED UNDER HIS HAT,
AND HIS MIDDLE NAME'S 'KURIOSITY'.
- SEGURAMENTE -
HEE-EE- ONLY KOKOKNUTTS
HAVING PEERED, HAVING PRIED
HAVING QUITE SATISFIED
⑥ HIS AMAZING AMOUNT OF 'KURIOSITY'
HE STARTS PURRING WITH PLEASURE,
EXULTS BEYOND MEASURE
WITH A TUNEFUL OUTBURST OF VERBOSITY.
=VERILY =
FEAR.
FATE
⑦
OH FATE: MYSTERIOUS MISTRESS OF OUR LIVES
A 'KAT' HERE ON THY BOUNTY THRIVES
AND A 'MOUSE'S' VILLAINY BECOMES THE BUTT
OF JAMES, AND JOSEPH KOKOKNUTT -
SIN DUDA
KELLY'S BRICK-YARD.
?
ONE SIDE ONE SIDE !!
⑧ THAT VILLAIN'S SPEED IS IN THE HIGHEST GEAR
WHOSE HEART IS THROWN INTO THE CLUTCH OF FEAR.
= Y'DERNTOOTTIN.
MY DAY-DREAM WAS OF 'IGNATZ: L'IL AINJIL - AND I'M A HEPPY, HEPPY KET'.
⑨ YES, IT WAS
- THE WIND THAT BLEW FROM THE SOU-SOU-WEST
THAT TOSSED JIM, AND JOE. KOKOKNUTT OUT OF THEIR NEST.
• BUT • HIS DAUGHTER —— MISS 'ZEPHYR' WITH HER SONG FROM THE WEST
LULLS 'JIMMY,' AND JOEY,' GENTLY TO REST.
= ADIOS =
10
HERRIMAN

JULY 2, 1916

CHIMNEY BUTTES.
"IGNATZ MOUSE" IS LOST !! LOST ON THE DESERTS OF "COCONINO" !!
"IGNATZ I BRING YOU A "MAGIC JUG"
NOW THAT YOU ARE BLIND FOLDED, MAKE A "GOOD RESOLUTION", SCRATCH THREE TIMES UPON THE "JUG", AND HELP WILL BE AT HAND
?
ADIOS.
ABOUT AS GOOD A RESOLUTION AS I COULD MAKE WOULD BE TO RESOLVE NOT TO THROW "BRICKS" AT "KRAZY KAT" ANY MORE
SCRATCH SCRATCH SCRATCH
WAL WA-AL START THE "MAGIC" COME ON, START IT !!
AH-H SOMETHING'S COMMENCING NOW
M-MH-
SAVED, L'IL DAHLINK HE'S SAVED !!
AND THAT NIGHT, "KRAZY'S" RAMBLE ACROSS THE SANDS OF THE "DESIERTO PINTADO" WAS LONG, AND ARDUOUS.
THE FOLLOWING MORNING...
AH, IT CAN'T BE HIM, HE'S LOST ON THE "DESERT"
IT LOOK'S LIKE HIM.
IT IS TOO HIM, I CAN SEE BETTER'N YOU FELLAS, I'M NEARER UP TO HIM -
MY-MY-MY.
YES ?
AND I MADE A GOOD RESOLUTION, SCRATCHED THE JUG THREE TIMES, AND HERE I AM -
WHAT WAS THE GOOD RESOLUTION, "IGNATZ" ?
YES, WOT WAS IT ?
OH
HA
HUH
OH, HELLO!, "IGNATZ" I'M SO GLED YOU ARE SAFE -
OOY
UM
OH HOH
!
SO YOU MADE A GOOD RESOLUTION ?
YES, AND I INTEND TO KEEP IT.
L'IL AINJIL !!
HERRIMAN

JULY 9, 1916

AS I LOOK ABOUT ME TO-NIGHT, AND GAZE UPON THIS VAST, AND INTELLIGENT AUDIENCE, I CAN READ IN IT'S EYE THE MESSAGE OF IT'S MIND, THE ONE BIG IDEA, THE ONE SOLID CONCEPTION, THE ONE CONCRETE BELIEF - "PRE-PAREDNESS" BURSTING INTO LIFE - ETC -
HEAR HEAR.
I WILL NOW TAKE THE "AUDIENCE" INTO MY INNERMOST CONFIDENCE - - AUDIENCE LOOK WELL UPON THIS -
YIZZA.
I WILL ALSO ASK THE AUDIENCE, HAS IT A "ENEMY"?
YIZZA, I HAVE, BUT, OH HE'S SUCH A SWEET LIL' ENEMY - HE'S SO NICE -
BEWARE OF SUCH A "ENEMY" !! HE STRIKES IN THE DARK !!! BUT, WITH MY "LITTLE GEM VANISHER" YOU NEED FEAR NO ENEMY - ONE THRUST OF THE HEAD, THUS, AND BEHOLD YOU ARE INVISIBLE TO THE WORLD, AND YOUR ENEMY !!
OOY-
THE "LITTLE GEM VANISHER" IS NOT A STATIONARY ARTICLE, IT MOVES, IT TRAVELS, IT TAKES YOU ABOUT, FROM PLACE TO PLACE UNSEEN, AND INVISIBLE!
I WONDER IF REALLY I DONT SEE HIM, OR NOT ?
AND FOR 60 CENTS THIS LITTLE ARTICLE OF SAFETY IS YOURS -
"SIXTY CENTS" AH-HAH, I THOUGHT THEY WAS A "JOKA" IN THE DECK, SOMEWHERES !!
60¢
HUH- 60¢
60¢- ROBBA, !! BECK ELLIES IS FULL OF "VANISHERS" AND HERE I AM INWISIBLE FREE FOR NOTHING -
OH- HOH
BA-AM!
ZIP
DONT EVER KEEP ME WAITING TWO HOURS FOR YOU AGAIN !! KRAZY KAT !!
NOT ONLY A ROBBA, BUT ALSO A "FIBBA" !!
ZIP
NEVER A-GAIN WILL I BE A "INTELLIGENT AUDIENCE" !!
HERRIMAN

JULY 15, 1916

"WILLIAM BEE" ALIAS "BUM BILL" —
A LABORER, A DRONE, A VAGABOND,
WITHOUT A HOME, WITHOUT A WIFE,
HE HAS NO ENEMY, HE HAS NO FRIEND —
CONTINUED IN LOWER RIGHT HAND CORNER.
HELP, HELP !!
HELP, HELP !!
I'M CAMINK, I'M CAMINK !!
HELP !!
GRAB A-HOLD, ATTA BEE —
I GOT IT —
YOU'VE GOT NO IDEA HOW THANKFUL I AM TO YOU, "KRAZY," I WAS DOWN FOR THE THIRD TIME TOO —
OH, DUNT MENTION IT MR. BEE, BY ME IT ALSO WAS A PLEASURE I INSURE YOU —
RIGHT OVER THE PLATE —
ZIP
I GOT HIM —
AH-H-H "IGNATZ" IS NIGH,
ZIZZ BUZZ-ZZ ZUZZ ZZZ BZEE ZUMM BZAA PSMM ZMM BZMM BMM
"AINJIL MICE"
— HE IS A CHILD OF DESTINY WITHOUT A DESTINATION, A PILGRIM ON THE ROAD TO "NOWHERE."
— "SAY TOO"
HERRIMAN

JULY 22, 1916

HURRY HOME WITH THAT "SOAP" KRAZY, YOUR "AUNT TABBY" NEEDS IT RIGHT AWAY.
GROCER
YIZZA.
TA DA DA-DAAA
OD-ZIGGETY-
I CALL THIS RATHA KLEEVA, I DO-
GOSH !!
OOY-
LOOKOW, LOOOO-KOW !!
HIS DOOM IS AT HAND. !!
NO "MOUSE" CAN WALK ON MY FACE, AND LIVE.
HALT.
OH, I'LL GETCHA-
GEEVIM, GEEVIM.
AH- MY "SOAP," FOR ONCE IN HIS LIFE, "KRAZY" GOT A MOVE ON HIMSELF.
ZIPS
GOODY, GOODY.
PHLEBOTOMY HAS BEEN PERFORMED UPON HIS NOSE.
OMY OMY.
SPARE HIM, "ENTIE." OH SPARE THE LITTLE DAHLINK.
MIZZABIL MOUSE-
WHAT DANGEROUS EYES YOU'VE GOT, MISS "TABBY."
OH, OFFISSA "PUPP," QUIT YOUR KOODAFOODLIN-
POOR L'IL AINJIL.

JULY 29, 1916

AUGUST 6, 1916

AUGUST 13, 1916

AUGUST 20, 1916

AUGUST 27, 1916

SEPTEMBER 3, 1916

SEPTEMBER 10, 1916

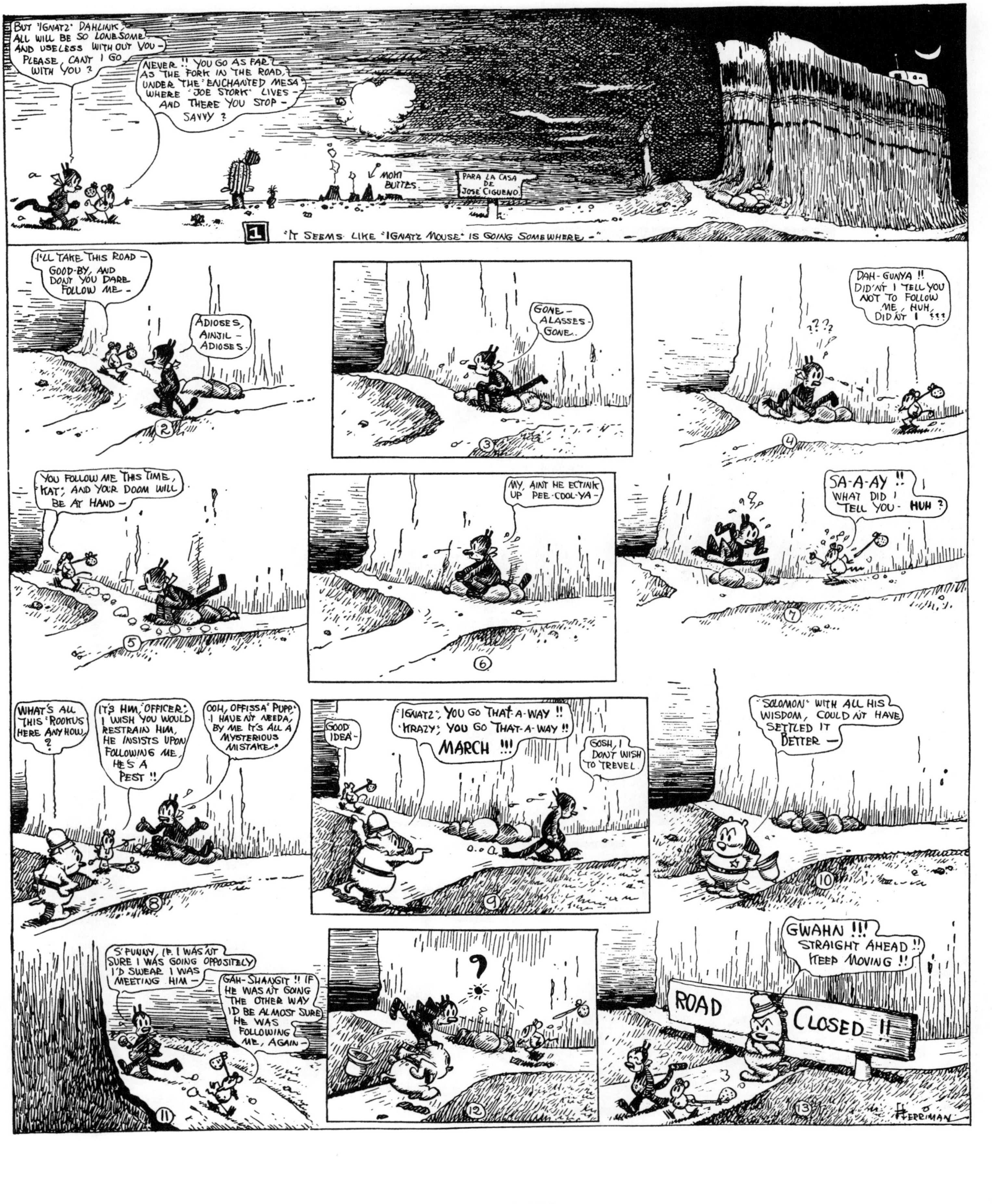

SEPTEMBER 17, 1916

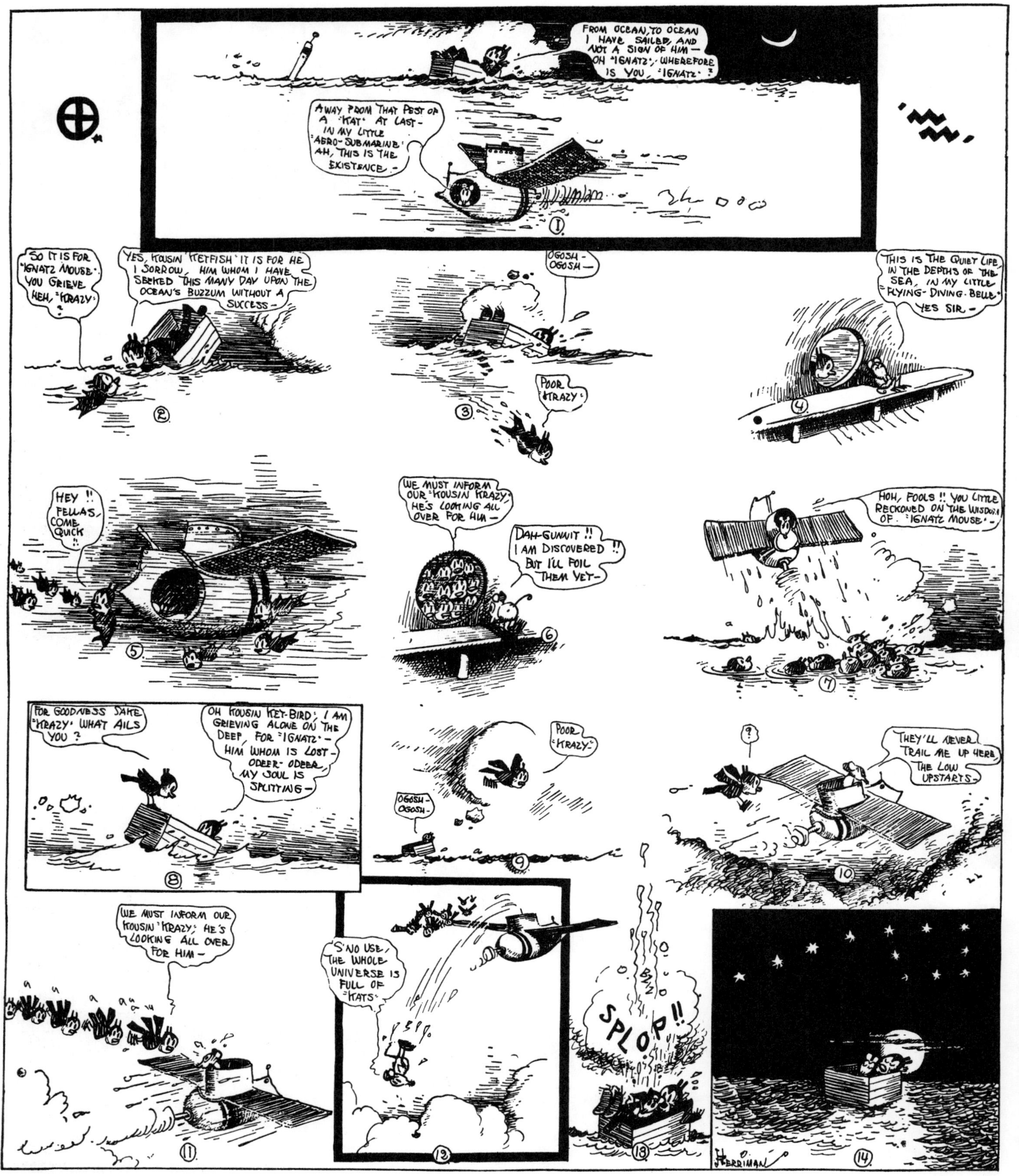

SEPTEMBER 24, 1916

OCTOBER 1, 1916

OCTOBER 8, 1916

OCTOBER 15, 1916

OCTOBER 22, 1916

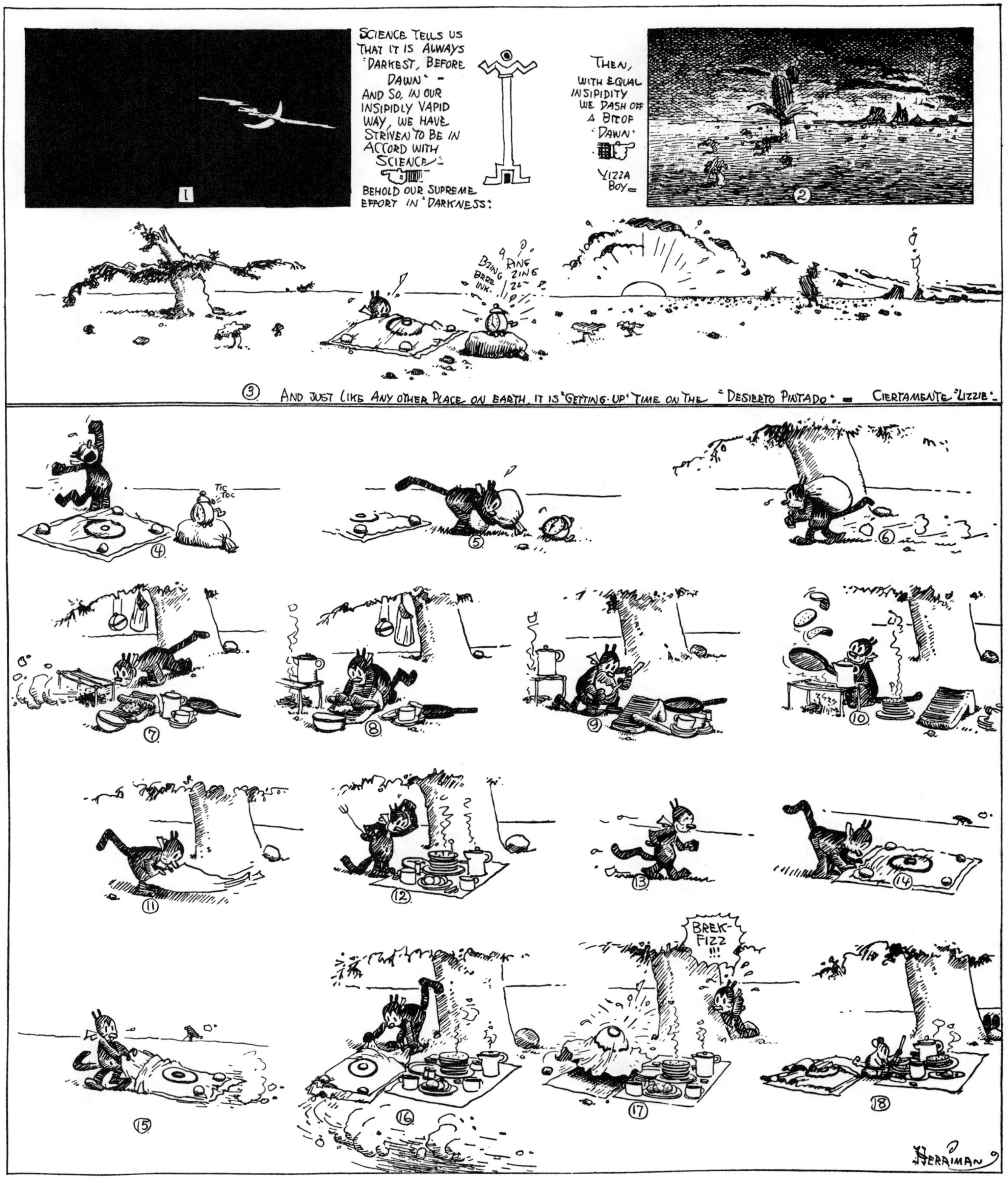

OCTOBER 29, 1916

NOVEMBER 5, 1916

NOVEMBER 12, 1916

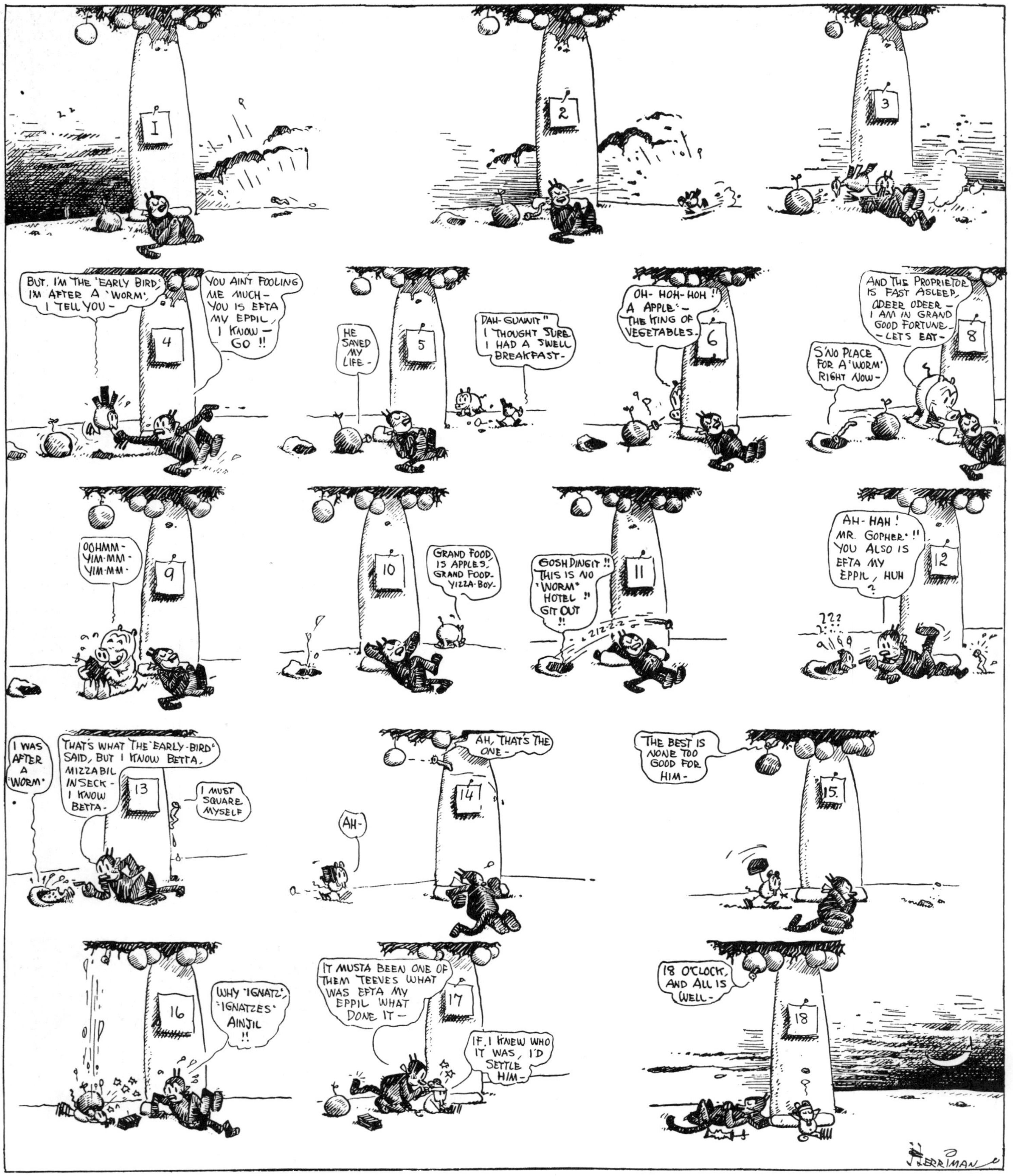

NOVEMBER 19, 1916

NOVEMBER 26, 1916

DECEMBER 3, 1916

DECEMBER 10, 1916

DECEMBER 17, 1916

DECEMBER 24, 1916

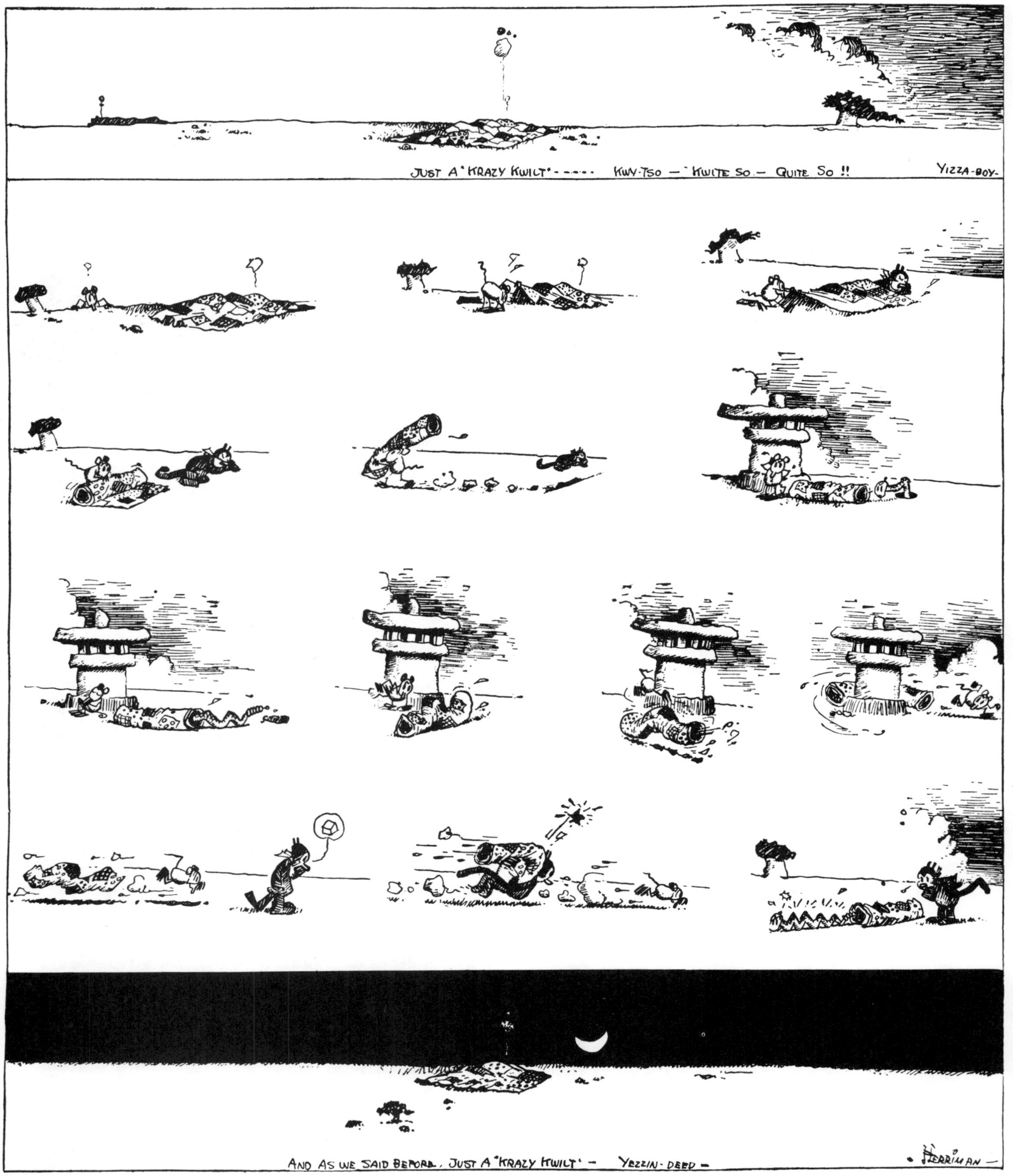

DECEMBER 31, 1916

The Kat Maker

George Herriman

1880—1944

There was a lot of Dickens in him, a lot of Lewis Carroll, a lot of W.C. Fields and vaudeville and low-life comedy, and just as obviously a lot of Eliot and Joyce and Ubu Roi.

But George Herriman was ultimately a hundred and eighteen and a half coconino per cent his own man, a man who would have undoubtedly lifted his eyebrows at the mention of those names, all of which are much more present in our assessment of the artist than they probably were in his own view of himself — a view that seems to have been modest to the point of self-effacement.

Herriman would have certainly liked the Dickens and Carroll and Fields analogies — and he would have sparked a grin at the inclusion of Chaplin and Laurel and Hardy as well — but he might have boggled a bit at the others.

It is a strange thing to say about a cartoonist so revered and widely known in his own time, but Herriman's intellectuality remains still unplumbed.

We have sparkling letters from him to the lowest of risque gag-cartoon magazines of the 1920s, comic reviews of Chaplin films in movie magazines (written as if by Krazy), but not a signed word by him in the heavyweight literary and artistic periodicals of his epochal period in the arts.

Vanity Fair put him in its Hall of Fame and got him to do a Sunday-style Kat page for one of its 1930s issues, but garnered not a line of non-comic prose or verse from this shy master.

The fine-tooth-comb research on the cartoonist's life set forth in the recent Harry Abrams Krazy Kat volume elicits no hint of his reading or visual interests.

We know he loved to visit the old Mack Sennet studios in Hollywood and put his feet up and gas with the directors and comics, but we don't know what galleries he frequented, or what books crammed his shelves.

We don't even know his response to the Armory Show — even though it contained a painting by Rudolph Dirks of "Katzenjammer Kids" fame.

All we have is Krazy Kat itself.

All we have, in short, is a universe of fantasy and poetry and the wildest comedy this side of Charley Chase and the Marx Brothers.

In the end, Krazy Kat tells us all we need to know about Herriman.

Herriman's father, variously a barber, a baker, and a tailor, had the foresight to move his family (including George, then six years old) from the creole poetry of New Orleans to the cinematic golden mean of sun-dappled Los Angeles in 1886.

REAL AMERICA, MAY 1934

Success in California

Above: George Herriman in the Hollywood Hills, with Krazy, and his beloved duo of scotties. *Facing Page and Overleaf:* Early examples of Major Ozone art.

As soon as he could, George skipped out of the apprenticeship to whichever of his father's Micawberish occupations was then turning up to pursue his own way with pen and ink and what was to become the most wholly individual comic graphic imagination of the twentieth century.

It seemed at first that there was nothing that Herriman could draw that wouldn't sell. One-shot comic-page layouts went into print at once in major newspapers; his gag cartoons garnered quick and welcome bucks from the *Judge* and *Life* humor magazines of the time.

George Herriman's tenative strip character ideas took hold and delighted readers on sight.

From "Professor Otto" and "Musical Mose" in 1902 he went on to "Lariat Pete" and "Two Jolly Jackies" in 1903, then to "Major Ozone" and "Bud Smith" and "Zoo Zoo" and "Baron Mooch" and "Alexander" and "The Dingbat Family" and there seemed to be no end. Even after he unknowingly entered into immortality with "Krazy Kat," he spun out more graphic fancies in "Baron Bean" and "Stumble Inn" and "Us Husbands" through the 1910s and 1920s.

And all of this work, every bit of it right down to the most casual effort, is a visual delight and a dithyramb of ebullient, subtly

MAJOR OZONE. WORLD PUBLISHING COMPANY, 1906

offbeat fancy that is simply unlike anything else in comic art before or since his time.

It is, of course, the work of genius.

Biographically, there really isn't much more to say.

Herriman's life was largely quiet and devoted to his family and his work.

He greatly enjoyed excursions to the great American desert he so deftly portrayed in his later work, in the company of such cartoonist buddies as Rudy Dirks, Jimmy Swinnerton, and "Rubbernose" Tom MacNamara.

He relished family life, and gloried in the considerable cartooning talent of his daughter, Bobbie.

He was tickled with Don Marquis' delirious "archy and mehitabel" books and wound up illustrating all three of them in a one-volume reissue edition that has now become a comic classic and a perfect wedding of author and artist talents.

He suffered through some poor film adaptions of Krazy Kat without being allowed to add the supervisory touch that might have made these films marvellous.

He corresponded a lot and bowled over friends and even first-time letter-writers with gifts of original watercolors, hand-tinted comic strip art he had had the good sense to retrieve from the syndicate slide-chutes to oblivion.

For George Herriman, it was a largely good and happy and obviously inspiring life.

— Bill Blackbeard

A Note from the Publishers As mentioned in the introduction to his volume, the problems of establishing a complete run of Sunday Krazy pages can prove to be a real nightmare for any enterprising archivist. As local editors invariably would break that run by pulling a page here and there, no Hearst newspaper archive offers the student a complete record of Herriman's achievement.

Once again we must thank Bill Blackbeard, and The San Francisco Academy of Comic Art. Culling together pages from a number of different Hearst papers, Blackbeard has in fact established perhaps the only complete run of all of the Krazy pages currently in existence. We will rely on the Blackbeard Collection almost exclusively in our own forthcoming volumes.